SPINALONGA

SPINALONGA

The Leper Island

Beryl Darby

EFSTATHIADIS GROUP

ISBN 960 226 109 9

Photography by the author and B. Vasiliades

New Impression 1993

Printed and bound in Greece by
EFSTATHIADIS GROUP S.A.

Distributed by
EFSTATHIADIS GROUP S.A.
HEAD OFFICE: AGIOU ATHANASIOU ST. GR - 145 65 ANIXI ATTIKIS
TEL: (01) 8140602, 8140702 FAX: (01) 8142915 TELEX: 216176 EF
ATHENS BRANCH: 14 VALTETSIOU ST. GR - 106 80 ATHENS
TEL: (01) 3633319, 3614312, 3637284 FAX: (01) 3614312
ATHENS BOOKSHOP: 84 ACADEMIAS ST. TEL: 3637439
THESSALONIKI BRANCH: 4 C. CRISTALLI ST. ANTIGONIDON SQUARE
THESSALONIKI, GR - 546 30 TEL: (031) 511781, 542498, FAX 544759
THESSALONIKI BOOKSHOP: 14 ETHNIKIS AMINIS ST. TEL: (031) 278158·

SPINALONGA – THE LEPER ISLAND

The island of Spinalonga lies in the Bay of Mirabello, Crete, approximately thirty kilometres from the town of Aghios Nikolaos. The name, Spinalonga, was given by the Venetians and means the 'Long Arm'.

The name aptly describes the peninsular which protrudes into the bay, making a safe and natural harbour which has been used since pre-Venetian times. The arm of land became an island when the French cut a small canal there in 1897.

At the end of the eight kilometres of land, separated by a narrow channel of water, is a much smaller island. It is thought that at one the time two islands were joined and only separated after volcanic activity or land slip in the remote past.

The larger island boasts a taverna and an hotel close to the canal cutting. There is also a mosaic floor depicting fish, from an early Christian Basilica; but the island's main claim to fame are its underwater remains of the town of Olous.

If a boatman can be persuaded to lower his mast and navigate the narrow, shallow canal it is possible to peer through the water and see large blocks of masonry lying on the sea bed. The finds from this sunken city are on show in the museum at Aghios Nikolaos and many of the artifacts are unique.

Of more interest to visitors to the area is the smaller island, which was the last leper colony in Europe. Numerous boat tours are run to the island, but there is a scarcity of information for those who wish to know more about its history.

Only one book is available on the subject, and although thoroughly enjoyable, it does not cover every aspect of the island. With this object in mind I have split this book into five small sections, together with a plan of the part of the island that was occupied by the lepers and hope that it will be a useful guide to future visitors.

I should also like to take the opportunity of thanking my step-daughter, through whom I was able to contact a leper who had spent many years on the island and who provided me with so much information about his life.

Neither must I forget my own two daughters who spent three days on Spinalonga with me, helping to measure the buildings and take notes. Without them it would have been an impossible task.

Map of Western Crete

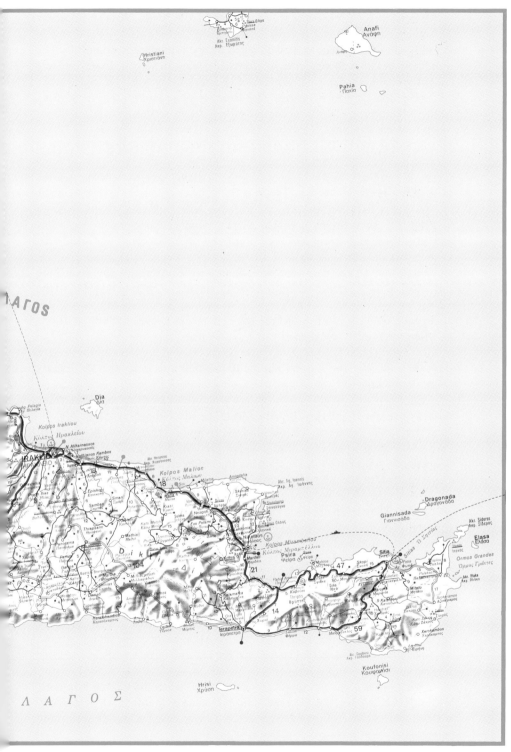

Map of Eastern Crete

HISTORY

The island of Crete is roughly equidistant from Africa, Asia and Europe. This unique situation was a great advantage to Crete for trading and also as the recipient of new ideas as they travelled from one continent to another. The disadvantages of such a position in the Mediterranean Sea was that Crete was sought after by all the great powers of the various ages.

After the Dorian invasions, the Romans conquered Crete in 66 B.C. having taken three years to accomplish the victory, so fierce was the defence put up by the Cretans.

In 395 A.D. the Roman Empire was divided into East and West. Crete became part of the Byzantine Empire until 824 A.D. when the Arab Saracens invaded from Spain and after conquering the island used it as a home base for their pirate raids.

It was a hundred and thirty five years before the Turks managed to dislodge the Saracens by laying siege to Chandrax for eight months. The treasure that had been amassed there by the Saracens was taken to Constantinople and once again Crete became part of the Byzantine Empire.

In 1204 A.D. the Crusaders who conquered Constantinople divided the provinces of the Byzantine Empire between themselves. Crete was sold to the Venetians by Boniface, the Marquis of Momferato, but before the Venetians could take possession of the island the Genoese occupied the key positions and regarded it as their own.

It was not until 1210 A.D. after many battles, that the Venetians were in a position to occupy the country and build fortifications to protect themselves from all comers.

The fortresses that they constructed were considered impregnable by the military experts of the day, but they were proved wrong.

The Turks attacked Chania and Rethymnon in 1645 A.D. and both fortresses surrendered. Heraklion was besieged for twenty one years until the town finally fell in 1669 A.D. marking the complete conquest of Crete with the exception of the island of Spinalonga.

Finally in 1715 A.D. the Turks laid siege to Spinalonga and were successful. They left a skeleton force on the island, who were later joined by their families and by 1830 A.D. there were eighty Mohammedan families living in the fort and in houses they had constructed themselves from the Venetian house remains.

During the next fifty years the population of the island increased to over a thousand families of Turkish descent, all engaged in the profitable occupation of smuggling.

In 1898 A.D. Crete was declared autonomous under the sovereignty of the Sultan. The majority of the Turks left the island in the same year, but those on Spinalonga refused to leave their homes and give up their lucrative business.

The position was tolerated until 1903 A.D. when the Cretan Republic, under Prince George, passed a resolution to make Spinalonga a leper colony. Fearful that lepers would be sent among them the Turks left the island immediately and have never attempted to return.

A map showing Ayios Nikolaos, Elounda Beach and Spinalonga

MAPS OF SPINALONGA DATED 1601

Taken from the book
Fortresses and Castles of Greece
by *A. Paradissis*

KEY

1. Tiepolo or Riva Rampart.
2. Bembo Pontoon.
3. Main Gate.
4. Genese Rampart.
5. Side Perina
6. Michiel Scarp.
7. Wooden Bridge.
8. Rangone Rampart.
9. Rampart Bondumier.
10. Dona Rampart.
11. Barbariga Scarp Veniera.
12. Moreta Square.
13. Mosta Square.
14. Carbonano Redan.
15. Gate.
16. Mema Curtain.
17. Fianco Molin.
18. Faliero Curtain.
19. Traversa Mora.
20. Mountain Gate.
21. Moceniga Square.
22. Miani.
23. Punta Veniera.
24. Venier Curtain.
25. Orsini Cavallier.
26. Grimani Curtain.
27. Contarini Redan.
28. Little Door.
29. Entrance to Island.

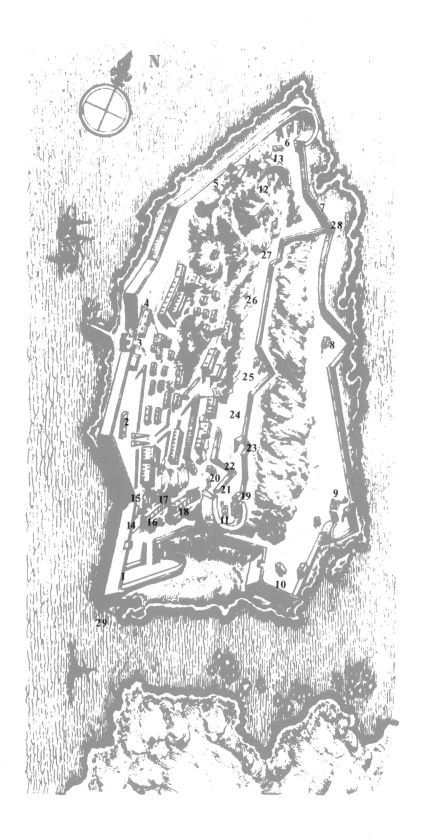

Remains of Michael Scarp.

THE VENETIAN FORT

Before the arrival of the Venetians on Crete there is reputed to have been a fortress on the small island of Spinalonga to protect the town of Olous and the harbour. Olous, most of which is now beneath the sea, was a collection centre for the salt produced from the mines at Elouda.

There are no visible remains of an older building, but all traces above ground would have been removed with the construction of the Venetian fort and any left below ground could only be found by the professional archaeologist.

Although the Venetians occupied Crete in 1210 A.D. they did not construct their fortress on Spinalonga until directed to do so by Jacopo Foscarini in 1579 A.D. If there was a fortress already on the island they may have considered that it gave sufficient defence to the area for three hundred and fifty years.

The foundation stone was laid on 15th June 1579 by the Provisor Generalis and there is a stone lintel above the gateway to the old port to commemorate the event. The two lines of inscription can just be deciphered and read:

LUCAS MIC(HAEL) PRO(VISOR) GE(NERALIS)
CR(ETAE) II AN(NO)

Entrance to the fort - lintel above arch carries inscription.

Above the inscription the sculptured white Venetian lion, the symbol of their power, still stands out clearly, although the weather is gradually taking its toll.

The huge granite rock, which is the island, was incorporated into the defences when the fort was constructed. To fully appreciate their skill it is necessary to sail around the island, where the other lion on the northern wall can also be seen.

The high defensive walls at the northern end of the island meet and marry into the rock face before dropping almost vertically to the sea, making an attack from that quarter impossible. The wall is built out into a semicircle, incorporating a cat walk, approximately eight feet wide, with gun emplacements below which face the open sea.

A little further to the east, where the approach from the sea is only slightly less steep the same construction occurs again.

As the land falls away in the south the massive walls curve inwards to form an entrance tunnel sixty four feet long, originally blocked by a stout wooden door on the seaward side. The tunnel both curves and narrows to the disadvantage of any attackers.

Once through the tunnel, having climbed the steps on the right, it is possible to scramble up a rough path to a narrow arch. Behind the arch is a narrow path that skirts the wall of the fort and a slight incline. At the top of the incline there is yet another archway which leads to the central and highest area of the fort.

A wide cat walk is approached by six deep steps to give an uninterrupted view across the Sea of Crete towards the island of Rhodes. Below the cat walk are gun emplacements strategically placed to give no quarter to any craft that should try to slip between the islands.

Returning to the gateway by the sea, after the last curve, where the water laps against the walls, the wall straightens to run northwards to the main gate where Foscarini laid the foundation stone. From there it continues in a straight line until it reaches the remains of an ammunition tower at the northern end.

In 1630 A.D. the fortress is reported as having thirty five cannon of various calibre and to be completely impregnable.

Apart from the fortifications built by the Venetians they also constructed water-sheds from the roofs of their buildings which conducted the rain water gradually downwards until it could be collected in the large tunnels that they had built. The openings to these tunnels can still be seen and it is advisable to take care when peering into the murky depths as there is nothing to prevent the unwary from falling into the dirty water some feet below.

The fort, built three hundred years ago, is in a very good state of preservation. Unfortunately it has become so overgrown that it would be dangerous to scramble too freely to investigate. There is always the possibility of a hidden hole or crumbling masonry where stone has been removed from a wall to effect a repair elsewhere.

Despite the air of neglect the fort will stand for many more years yet as a tribute to the Medieval builders.

LEPROSY

The disease of Leprosy, called Meslkinies by the Greeks, has always been one of the most feared diseases of ancient man. It has, since Biblical times, been considered to be a sign of impurity, and the unfortunate sufferers forced to live apart from the rest of the community.

Until the twentieth century the lepers on Crete were ostracized and forced to live as best they could in caves or shelters built by themselves, dependent upon the charity of the healthy members of their families for the necessities of life and the little that they could acquire from begging.

The disfigurement, pain and degradation brought about by the disease isolated them from a normal life.

The Norwegian physician, Armauer Hansen, discovered the leprosy bacillus in 1873, but although he could identify the germ in the body he did not know how it had been caught or how to cure it.

The Mycobacterium Leprae, when under a microscope, resembles the Tuberculosis Bacterium, being a slightly curved rod. The incubation period can be from three to five years, or even longer before there are any visible signs.

There are two kinds of leprosy bacteria, the Tuberculoid being a much milder form which is also self healing. The Lepromatous bacteria, being progressive, can take between ten and thirty years before causing visible open wounds.

The first indications are a whitening of the skin and the development of massive nodules. There is localised swelling of the nerves and extensive areas of anaesthesia in the skin. The swelling leads to cracking and bruising and the open wounds associated with the disease.

As the disease progresses the nerves which have been attacked in the first instances are destroyed and this, along with the absorption of the bone, causes the loss of fingers and toes.

For centuries the only known treatment was Chaulmoorga Oil. In 1941 a sulphone derivative was found to be effective for keeping the disease under control. 'Dapsone' when given orally over a long period of time gives a satisfactory response, although the body eventually builds up a resistance.

Rifampicin, Clofazimine and Thiacetazone are the most recent drugs being used in the treatment of leprosy and an experimental programme with B.C.G. vaccine is currently underway in Uganda. If the B.C.G. vaccine is successful it does seem possible that a full scale vaccination programme could be undertaken in the areas of the world where the disease is most prevalent.

If the disease is diagnosed early enough it is now possible to halt its progress without any serious deformity. Where deformity is feared physiotherepy can often be employed to prevent it and as a last resort for extreme cases plastic and orthopaedic surgery can be effective in allowing the sufferer to lead a normal life.

The only way to catch leprosy is through direct contact between an open wound on a leper and a fresh wound on a healthy person. Strangely enough males appear to be more susceptible to the disease than females, although it is not hereditary through the male line.

Dietary deficiencies seem to play no part in the disease, unlike scurvy and rickets, nor does the climate.

1000 A.D. to 1400 A.D. saw the highest concentration of lepers in Great Britain, the disease probably brought back during the Crusades, but certainly not killed off by a cooler climate.

The last case of British leprosy died in 1798 in the Shetland Isles; although almost two hundred years later, there are three hundred and sixty recorded cases of lepers living in Britain, all of whom came into the country already suffering from the disease and are receiving treatment.

The lepers who lived in Greece eighty years ago were not so fortunate.

THE LEPERS

When the island of Spinalonga was declared a leper colony by the Government in 1903 there was a mass exodus of the Turkish inhabitants.

The lepers who had been living in caves and shacks in various parts of Crete were gradually found and taken out to the island. They were expected to make their homes in the remnants of the Venetian fort and the Turkish and Venetian houses that were there.

In many respects they were far better off than they had been on the mainland. They were able to use the old hospital building for the most severely ill, although for four years they did not have a doctor to visit them and had to treat themselves as best they could.

There is no natural water supply on the island and fresh water and food were brought over from the mainland on a rather irregular basis.

Disheartened, disfigured, and often in tremendous pain, about four hundred men and women lived from day to day doing nothing to better their existence.

A short distance from Heraklion, in a village, a small boy played happily. For the purpose of this account I shall call him George. When he was nine his parents became worried about his skin condition and took him to the local doctor. The doctor carried out a series of tests, all of which were non-conclusive, although the doctor felt quite certain in his own mind that the boy had leprosy.

When George was seventeen, leprosy was finally diagnosed and he was sent to the Pasteur Institute in Athens where further tests were taken and he was given therapy. His condition gradually deteriorated and he was sent as incurable to the leper hospital.

The conditions in the hospital were not ideal to start with, but they rapidly worsened when a French Ambassador who was in Athens at the time, put forward a petition for all lepers in Greece to be confined in one hospital to lessen the risk of infection to outsiders.

More lepers were brought in from all over the country until each small ward

Elounda Beach

Spinalonga from across the Bay

A view of the ruins through an Arch

held sixty four patients. Very often the normal water supplies were exhausted and water was brought from other parts of Athens in filthy barrels, sometimes never arriving at all.

George decided that life in the hospital at that time was intolerable. Together with some of the other young men and women he went on hunger strike and refused to comply with the hospital authorities. Unlike today when their complaints would be investigated, green straight jackets were brought into the ward and the orderlies began to force the patients into them.

Despite their sickness and physical disabilities the lepers fought furiously until eventually the police were called in. Finally the ring leaders were safely installed in their jackets and promptly transferred to Spinalonga still wearing them.

With tremendous courage and endurance they began to build up a community with the help of the lepers who were already there. The new contingent of lepers were better educated than those who had lived in the caves and shacks on Crete. Many of them had been trained as lawyers, teachers or craftsmen, even the youngest having attended High School.

They organised themselves into small working parties and began a programme of renovation. They selected the least dilapidated of the houses and began to repair them, taking the necessary stones and timbers from the

A ghost street

One of the churches in the background

more tumble down homes. Where larger stones were needed the fittest amongst them would quarry them from the natural granite outcrop and transport them to the site.

To solve, to a certain extent, the problem of fresh water, the lepers copied the Venetian idea. They constructed water sheds from the roofs of their houses, which enabled them to collect rainwater in pots and buckets, and transported it to tanks which were situated at the far end of the island on a small hill.

Water was very important to the lepers. Although soap and water was painful for the sufferers, it was essential that they kept their bodies clean to lessen the risk of further infection in their open wounds.

Likewise their clothes and bandages had also to be kept clean and to this end they used the old Turkish laundry where there were open fireplaces to heat the water.

The women on the island always wanted more water than their ration allowed and they decided that the only way to solve the problem was to steal it. They would wait until after midnight and when most people were asleep they would creep up the hill with a bucket. Of course, it was not long before they were found out and the men put a guard on the water tanks.

Naturally the women knew about the guard and did not make their nocturnal trips so the guards became very bored. To relieve them of guard duty they invented a story about a ghost. The ghost began life as a Greek, but ended up as a Negro as the story was spread. The women, being very superstitious, believed the story for some weeks and kept away from the water tanks.

Although the lepers lived on Spinalonga it was still used as a convenient rendezvous for smugglers, particularly Italians. They would land on the island, off-load their goods, leaving one man behind to guard them whilst they rowed over to the mainland to negotiate with the buyers.

As the story of the ghost began to lose credence the women began to visit the water tanks again. One night as the women approached the tanks they received a terrible shock as a black man leapt out and began to wave.

The women fled back down the hill, screaming, leaving behind a very dark skinned and frightened Italian, who had mistaken the women for his companions returning after completing their business.

More and more people were being sent to the island and the older inhabitants gave then a sympathetic and friendly welcome. The community spirit had become very strong and help and encouragement was given to all. No one ever died alone, or lacked attention when they were bedridden, although often there was no doctor available.

There was the occasion when one of the women developed gangrene in her arm which necessitated amputation. The doctor was on the island at the time and performed the operation. George sat by her side, holding her other arm, stroking her forehead and talking to her, whilst the doctor sawed off the infected limb. There was no anaesthetic, no disinfectant and no clean bandages for her.

Quite often patients had to suffer amputation, the extreme cases having to lose all four limbs eventually. They never survived the final operation for very long, possibly due to shock or further infection.

The Government paid the lepers a pension of thirty drachmas per month. This sounds very little by todays standards, but then the purchasing power would have been far greater.

Many of them saved their money to help pay for a decent burial. This consisted of a wooden coffin, made by the island carpenter, and an individual grave with a wooden cross at the head. Those who had not saved enough and had no relatives to send money were placed in a deep cement tower at the end of the graveyard which acted as a mass grave.

It was the custom to remove the bodies from the individual graves after four years in order to re-use them as necessary, and it was at one of these four-yearly exhumations that a sad discovery was made.

A young girl of eighteen had arrived on the island. She was suffering from leprosy of the throat and whilst some accomodation was being made habitable for her she stayed with George and his wife.

The same evening as she arrived there was to be a dance in one of the tavernas and George asked her to accompany them and meet some of the other islanders. Being tired, and probably rather shy, she preferred to stay at their home. When they returned from the dance they found her collapsed on the floor having choked on an apple that she had been eating.

The funeral was arranged for the next day, although there was no doctor on the island at the time to certify her officially dead. Having brought money with her she was given an individual grave, but when the grave was disturbed, four years later, it was found that she had moved from the internment position. One arm was above her head and her face was turned to the side where she had struggled to get out.

Although life on the island was beset with difficulties, not the least of these being to stay alive and keep a deadly disease at bay, the lepers were cheerful and occupied their time much as any Greek on the mainland would.

Having helped each other to repair their houses, they laid out small gardens together, some choosing to have grass and flowers and others vegetable plots, yet others keeping lambs, goats, chickens etc. Young men and women met and married, eventually having healthy babies which the government took to an infant home in Athens where they were brought up away from infection.

Religious services were conducted regularly in the two orthodox churches that were on the island, the priest for one of them being a leper himself. Those who were able ran small shops distributing the produce that was sent from the mainland. There was even the barber and the hairdresser.

They built four tavernas where they could meet in the evenings and play backgammon, chess or cards beside a coal fire. They printed their own paper which was called the 'Satire' which had news of various events on the island, usually with a humorous twist.

One of the tavernas was also used as a small dance hall and they rented a projector to enable them to have film shows. This same taverna was used for the puppet shows which were called KARAGIOSI and had its origins in Asia Minor, the puppets being made out of wood and quite unlike European puppets.

A theatre group was also started and they performed their plays once a month, sending invitations out to the mainland villages and the local Mayor. The courageous inhabitants of the island began to be regarded with respect and no longer feared.

Relatives were permitted to visit whenever they wished and brought presents, personal possessions or goods that had been requested by the lepers. Every person and every item leaving the island had to go through the disinfection room, but this did not deter people from bringing small babies to be christened in the tiny church nearly opposite the port.

The lepers accepted their life on the island and were not unhappy there. Being cut off from the mainland caused communication difficulties as visitors had to be relied upon to post letters or take verbal messages to families. The delay was very frustrating if waiting for news of recovery from illness or to hear of a birth in the family.

When news had been delayed for a long period of time the islanders found the wait intolerable and would try to leave Spinalonga themselves. They would load up their wooden bath tubs with clean clothes, water and food and set out at night on a favourable wind, hoping to make a landing on the shore of Crete before daybreak.

George was successful in two such attempts to visit his family, but the escapades were discovered by the Governement and for a period of time the bath tubs were confiscated.

During the last war when Crete was occupied, there were no troops stationed on Spinalonga, but there were guards on the opposite shore. When the lepers tried to drift across the sea to obtain news of their families they were shot at by Germans and one man was killed.

It must not be thought that having placed the lepers on Spinalonga and provided them with a 'pension' of one drachma a day that the Authorities then forgot them.

Dr Grammatikakis, who became the Governor of Spinalonga in 1932 tried to better the living conditions of the lepers. It was at his instigation that the large concrete basins in the laundry area opposite the Church on the west side of the island were built.

An electric generator was sent out to the island and placed just outside the fortress walls. Every house on the island had the benefit of electric light before many of the villages on the mainland.

In 1937 a new hospital and laboratory were built up on the hill overlooking the community, and it was arranged that doctors and technicians would commute from the mainland to enable the lepers to have better medical treatment. Unfortunately this did not work out quite as well as it had been hoped. The facilities were there, but the necessary medical supplies were in very short supply, sometimes non-existent. At times, neither supplies nor doctors were able to reach the island due to bad weather.

Outside of the
Disinfection Room.

The Hospital.

The last house before the laundry with fourteen steps leading to the roof.

Finally in 1948, the Government built two blocks of flats, two storeys high. Each block contained twenty four single rooms and four kitchens. The more recent arrivals were usually allocated a room in the flats as the older inhabitants of the island preferred their original homes which reflected the personality of the occupant.

Before the last war the Greek Government had planned to extend the leper colony to incorporate the arm of land opposite the small island. The building of the flats had been the first phase of the plan and it was also to be the last.

By 1954 it was decided that all the lepers should be moved back to a hospital in Athens. Negotiations dragged on, and finally in 1957 the thirty lepers who were still alive, were moved back to the mainland hospital, George being amongst them.

The lepers were sad to leave their island and the mainlanders had to bid farewell to their friends and customers. On arriving at the hospital the lepers found that conditions had changed beyond belief. For many of them the disease had halted and they were able to accept responsible positions inside the hospital, thereby contributing to the community as they had in the past. After a few months none of them wished to return to Spinalonga.

Maybe George was luckier than most. He has a good job in the hospital and has married again, but he will never forget the years that he spent as an outcast from society on an island.

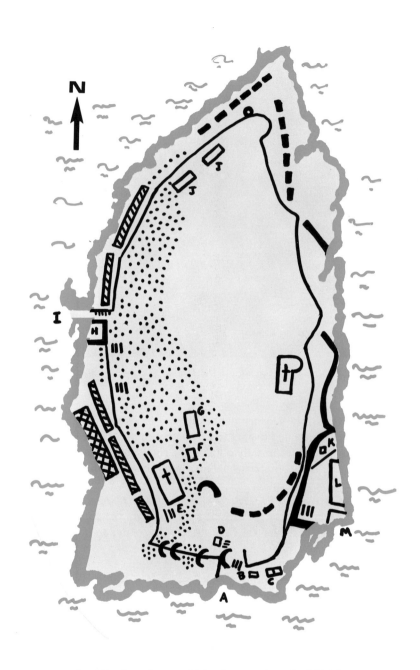

Length of road around island approximately 3,000 ft.

KEY

■ Venetian Construction.
▬ Modern Construction.
▨ Venetian Water Tunnels.
▧ Laundry.
A. Concrete Jetty.
B. Concrete Generator Base.
C. Cinema.
D. Re-constructed House.
E. Quarry Area.
F. Dispensary.
G. Hospital.
H. Disinfection Room.
I. Original Port and Entrance.
J. Flats.
K. Charnal House.
L. Graveyard.
M. Carpenter's House.
▒ Area Occupied by Lepers

The Dispensary.

31

THE WALK

As you approach the island of Spinalonga in a small motor boat the buildings begin to emerge as separate houses dotted over the island, but almost disappear from view as the boatman ties up at the tiny jetty, so high are the walls of the Venetian fort.

Outside the walls, on the right of the quay, is a large concrete rectangle, almost overgrown with weeds, where the electric generator stood when the island was occupied by the lepers.

Mount the few shallow steps that lead up straight in front of you and turn to the left, entering the tunnel that leads inside the walls of the fort. The tunnel itself is sixty four feet long and supported by eight arches, finally ending up one foot wider inside the walls than it was on the outer side.

Stop there, just for a moment and gaze around. On the right, half way up a flight of steps that lead to the upper part of the fortress, a two storeyed house has been repaired and given new shutters, balcony and door. It gives an idea how the houses would have looked when they were occupied.

At the bottom of the steps a concrete path has widened out to form a small square. Next to the tunnel entrance, behind you, there is a Venetian drinking fountain set into the wall and opposite the steps, on the left, is the first house in the colony. The weather-beaten wooden door is half open and you can look through into the far room, all of which is overgrown with a tangle of weeds.

Next to this house there was once a small path that led around to the rear of the building and it is still possible to negotiate the stinging nettles to arrive at the rear and climb the steps to a flat roofed area that runs across the top of the tunnel.

The house next door, in my opinion, is the prettiest on the island. Arched windows, once painted red, are on either side of an arched doorway, with the remains of a balcony running the width of the facade. Whoever decided to repair the house and live there kept the style of the original designers and builders and saw no need for exterior improvement.

Unfortunately next to it a concrete doorway has been erected and clearly marked with the number 19. A shop front, with long double doors, the bolt to fasten them still working, lean out drunkenly towards the street. The shutter next to them is still in working order, being hinged to fold back externally, the hook to hold it still in place.

Opposite, on the right, another shop front, the shutters fallen, yawns darkly into the sunshine. The yucca tree, probably planted originally as a seedling, has grown to cover half the house and path, and stretching to the archway over the road which used to be an integral part of the fort.

After the archway the houses continue on both sides of the road. Look into each of them and you will see the small domestic touches that still remain. A cupboard at ceiling level with the doors hanging open, an old basket gradually decaying on a shelf. The stairs at the side or in the back rooms lean drunkenly as their supports sag and the timbers rot.

The walls show traces of blue or yellow plaster, and in some houses a blue frieze has been run around the room at waist height. The tavernas are distinguishable by the wide arches leading to their back rooms where the large open fireplaces are clearly visible.

Number 29, (the number is on the door and it is next to the shop that was originally painted a brilliant cobalt blue), was obviously found to be draughty by the taverna customers as cardboard has been pinned on the inside of the floor and below the windows to act as a draught excluder.

The shutters have the date 1940 scratched on the inside and on the exterior letters TETRE–AOE–are just visible above faint carvings of small ships.

The last house in the row on the left side has fourteen stone steps which led to the flat roof and possibly another small room, long since fallen away.

This is the end of the little terrace of shops and tavernas where the lepers worked much as they would have done on the mainland had they been healthy. No doubt during the day there would have been little difference between this street on the island and any other street anywhere in Greece.

Returning to the archway and looking on the right, the first two houses are reasonably intact, but after that there are only side walls standing. The facades have completely disappeared, or may have been deliberately dismantled to provide building materials. At the end of the collapsed buildings there is a flight of wide, shallow steps leading up to the area that was used to quarry the stone as it was needed. Large , rough hewn blocks still lay there in irregular heaps.

A further flight of steps on the far side of the quarry are beside the tiny white-washed Church that was used for festive religious occasions and where the marriages and christenings took place. Unfortunately the Church has been robbed in the past and is now kept locked.

Opposite the Church runs the first of the Venetian water tunnels with seven steps leading up to the inspection chambers in two places. Between the old wall of the fort and the Venetian water tunnel is the site of the laundry. Here are the twenty four concrete basins that Dr Grammatikakis ordered to improve the washing facilities for the lepers.

The laundry was divided into two rooms, the first containing fourteen basins with six fireplaces for heating water, and the second with ten basins and four fires. The four supports that held the roof in position are still standing firmly, but the door that was in the dividing wall and the roof itself has disappeared.

Continuing from the Church on the right there are more houses, two of them having adjoining outbuildings, which, when investigated are found to be ground level toilets. Bordering the road here are arches and gateways which give on to secluded gardens, once well tended, but now looking like miniature jungles. These are the older Venetian houses. At the bottom of the gardens, the entrance being inside the walls, are the toilets. They were built with curved walls which project out onto the road. Once inside the overgrown garden you can peep through the narrow doorway and see the remains of wooden seats still in place.

Reconstruction House.

The first house.

The Square.

The second house - opposite the steps and reconstructed house.

The top half of the second house.

The 'prettiest' house.

The toilets on the other side of the road cannot be investigated, but can be distinguished, in many cases by their circular design and the lush green grass that grows over them.

Continue up the road, looking into every doorway to discover doors hanging on one hinge, shutters sagging, stairs leaning to one side, remnants of decoration or the timbers that once supported an upper floor lying in an untidy broken heap on the ground. There is an undefinable air of sadness as you gaze at the last remains of the lepers' homes.

At the very end of the row on the left side there is a large sturdy building. The window beside the road is of conventional height, but when you look through the ground level is far below. The room was originally part of the Venetian fort and was utilised by the Health Authorities as the Disinfection Room. Every bottle, jar, box and person that returned to the mainland had to go through the room.

Beside the Disinfection Room are the steps leading down to the old port that was used by the Venetians, the Turks and finally the lepers. If you walk down them and across the quay to the sea and turn and look up at the arch the inscription and the white Venetian lion mentioned earlier can be seen.

On the other side of the old port entry there is another Venetian water tunnel, again the inspection chambers being reached by two flights of steps. At the end of the tunnel is a patch of modern concrete and a small wooden outhouse, which yields no clue as to its former purpose, but stand there quietly and look at the opposite side of the road.

The gardens have become completely wild and overgrown with no one to tend them. Geraniums, roses and daisies grow in profusion against a background of trees and ruined buildings. Look upwards and a blocked window gives the illusion of a man standing there. The breeze makes a shutter bang and the rustling of a lizard in the undergrowth adds to the atmosphere. Are you completely alone on the island?

From there the houses that continue on the left side of the road are of more modern construction. But if you look carefully at the first house, (possibly the one where George and his wife lived), poked amongst the stones are rags, a sad reminder that the lepers had to use whatever was available to improve their conditions. These rags were no doubt pushed into holes and cracks to stop the draught and are still in situ thirty years later.

The houses continue, in various stages of collapse, on both sides of the road for some yards before the large, concrete flats rise on the right. There are two separate blocks, the first with a pale blue wash on the exterior and the second with a cream wash. The colour was the only difference between them.

Mount the steps which lead to the open doorway and just inside can be seen the remains of the concrete spiral staircase and the tiled cooking area. In the second block the same can be seen, but the light brackets are still in place on the wall and the remains of small circular tables are scattered on the concrete floor.

The flats are so out of keeping with the rest of the dwellings on the island that it is no surprise that the lepers were not very enthusiastic about them.

The fallen house next to the quarry. The prepared blocks of stone can be seen in the foreground.

Fallen house with overgrown garden.

The modern flats.

View of the flats - showing the old and new type of building.

From here climb the steps between the flats and look back along the hillside to see the hospital and the dispensary, both of which were built in 1937, again with the liberal use of concrete. It is no longer possible to climb up to them, as all the paths that once led there are completely overgrown.

Re-trace your steps back down to the road and continue to follow it around the island. Pass the ammunition tower at the north west corner and gaze down the sheer walls of the fort to the clear sea below. At the northern end of the island the fort stretches out below, inviting exploration, but not offering any safe access from above.

Continue down the east side of the island until another small Church comes into view on the right hand side. It was robbed at the same time as the other Church and is now kept locked. It was from this Church that the lepers conducted their burial service and subsequent internment.

Whilst we were on the island we were fortunate to see inside this Church when a family arrived from the mainland. They opened and cleaned the Church before lighting candles and saying a short prayer, presumably for a loved one who had perished on Spinalonga.

A few yards further on from the Church a flight of steps leads off on the seaward side. Follow these up to the graveyard where the small area contains forty four concrete graves, laid out in a grid pattern.

All the graves are of a regular size and with an even distance between them. The stone slabs that once covered them have been removed and it is possible to see a few bones and pieces of wood, the only visible remains of the last lepers to have been buried there before the return to Greece.

In the graveyard area there is a small building which was used by the island carpenter, himself a leper, as a workshop. In it he used to make the coffins and the crosses for those who wanted a decent burial.

Walk to the end of the series of graves, passing one large grave beside the wall, until there is a small opening between the graveyard wall and the wall of the fort. Step over the hole in the ground, which may have been another grave, and a few steps lead to a concrete tower.

In this tower, lying twelve feet down in the darkness, are the remains of the lepers who could not afford an individual grave, and those who were exhumed after four years. There is a small window let into the side at ground level and it is possible to look down and distinguish the skulls and long bones of over three hundred and eighty lepers.

This was the final resting place of all but thirty of the lepers who lived on Spinalonga; people whose bravery in the face of adversity and disease should never be forgotten.

The Graveyard.